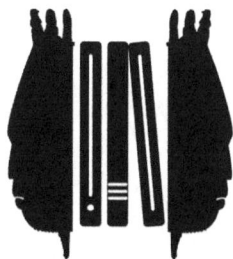

BLACK LEGACY PRESS™

WWW.BLACKLEGACYPRESS.ORG

SLAVE NARRATIVES

VOLUME VI
KANSAS NARRATIVES

By
United States.
Work Projects Administration

ISBN: 978-1-63652-225-8

SLAVE NARRATIVES

A Folk History of Slavery in the United States.
From Interviews with Former Slaves

UNITED STATES.
WORK PROJECTS ADMINISTRATION

TYPEWRITTEN RECORDS PREPARED BY
THE FEDERAL WRITERS' PROJECT
1936-1938
ASSEMBLED BY
THE LIBRARY OF CONGRESS PROJECT
WORK PROJECTS ADMINISTRATION
FOR THE DISTRICT OF COLUMBIA
SPONSORED BY THE LIBRARY OF
CONGRESS

WASHINGTON 1941

VOLUME VI
KANSAS NARRATIVES

**Prepared by
The Federal Writers' Project of
The Works Progress Administration
For the State of Kansas**

CONTENTS

THE AMERICAN GUIDE
TOPEKA, KANSAS

EX SLAVE STORY
OTTAWA, KANSAS
BY: Leta Gray (interviewer)

CLAYTON HOLBERT

"My name is Clayton Holbert, and I am an ex slave. I am eighty-six years old. I was born and raised in Linn County, Tennessee. My master's name was Pleasant "Ples" Holbert. My master had a fairly large plantation; he had, I imagine, around one hundred slaves."

"I was working the fields during the wind-up of the Civil War. They always had a man in the field to teach the small boys to work, and I was one of the boys. I was learning to plant corn, etc. My father, brother and uncle went to war on the Union side."

"We raised corn, barley, and cotton, and produced all of our living on the plantation. There was no such thing as going to town to buy things. All of our clothing was homespun, our socks were knitted, and everything. We had our looms, and made our own suits, we also had reels, and we carved, spun, and knitted. We always wore yarn socks for winter, which we made. It didn't get cold, in the winter in Tennessee, just a little frost was all. We fixed all of our cotton and wool ourselves."

"For our meat we used to kill fifteen, twenty, or fifty, and sometimes a hundred hogs. We usually had hickory. It was considered the best for smoking meat, when we butchered. Our meat we had then was the finest possible. It had a lot more flavor than that which you get now. If a person ran out of meat, he would go over to his neighbor's house, and borrow or buy meat, we didn't think about going to town. When we wanted fresh meat we or some of the neighbors would kill a hog or sheep, and would divide this, and then when we butchered we would give them part of ours. People were more friendly then then they are now. They have almost lost respect for each other. Now if you would give your neighbor something they would never think of paying it back. You could also borrow wheat or whatever you wanted, and you could pay it back whenever you thrashed."

"We also made our own sorghum, dried our own fruits. We usually dried all of our things as we never heard of such a thing as canning."

"We always had brandy, wine, and cider on hand, and nothing was thought of it. We used to give it to the children even. When we had corn husks, log rolling, etc., we would invite all of the neighbors over, and then we would serve refreshments of wine, brandy or cider."

"We made our own maple syrup from the maple sugar trees. This is a lot better than the refined sugar people have nowdays, and is good for you too. You can't get this now though, except sometimes and it is awfully high priced. On the plantations the slaves usually had a house of their own for their families. They usually built their houses in a circle, so you didn't have to go out doors hardly to go to the house next to you. If you wanted your house away from the rest of the houses, they could build you a house away from the others and separate."

I was never sold, I always had just my one master. When slave owners died, if they had no near relatives to inherit their property, they would 'Will' the slaves their freedom, instead of giving them to someone else. My grandmother, and my mother were both freed like this, but what they called 'nigger traders' captured them, and two or three others, and they took them just like they would animals, and sold them, that was how 'Ples' Holbert got my mother. My grandmother was sent to Texas. My mother said she wrote and had one letter from my grandmother after that, but she never saw her again."

"My mother used to be a cook, and when she was busy cooking, my mistress would nurse both me and her baby, who was four weeks older than me. If it happened the other way around, my mother would nurse both of us. They didn't think anything about it. When the old people died, and they left small orphan children, the slaves would raise the children. My young master was raised like this, he has written to me several times, since I have been out here in Kansas, but the last time I wrote, I have had no reply, so I suppose he was dead."

"When anyone died, they used to bury the body at least six feet under the ground. There wasn't such a thing as a cemetery then, they were just buried right on the plantation, usually close to the house. They would put the body in a wagon, and walk to where to bury the person, and they would sing all of the way."

"The slaves used to dance or go to the prayer meeting to pass their time. There were also festivals we went to, during the Christmas vacation. There was always a big celebration on Christmas. We worked until Christmas Eve and from that time until New Year's we had a vacation. We had no such thing as Thanksgiving, we had never heard of such a thing."

"In August when it was the hottest we always had a vacation after our crops were all laid by. That was the time when we usually had several picnics, barbecues or anything we wanted to do to pass our time away."

"After the war was over, and my father, brother and uncle had gone to war, it left my mother alone practically. My mother had always been a cook, and that was all she knew, and after the war she got her freedom, she and me, I was seven or eight years old, and my brother was fourteen, and my sister was about sixteen. My mother didn't know what to do, and I guess we looked kind of pitiful, finally my master said that we could stay and work for him a year, people worked by the year then. We stayed there that year, and then we also stayed there the following year, and he paid us the second year. After that we went to another place, Roof Macaroy, and then my sister got married while we were there, and then she moved on her husband's master's place, and then we went too. After that I moved on another part and farmed for two or three years, and then we moved to another part of the plantation and lived there three or four years. That was almost the center of things, and we held church there. All of the colored people would gather there. The colored people who had been in the North were better educated than the people in the South. They would come down to the South and help the rest of us. The white people would also try to promote religion among the colored people. Our church was a big log cabin. We lived in it, but we moved from one of the large rooms into a small one, so we could have church. I remember one time after we had been down on the creek bank fishing, that was what we always did on Sunday, because we didn't know any better, my master called us boys and told us we should go to Sunday school instead of going fishing. I remember that to this day, and I have only been fishing one or two times since. Then I didn't know what he was talking about, but two or three years later I learned what Sunday school was, and I started to go."

"I went to a subscription school. We would all pay a man to come to teach us. I used to work for my room and board on Saturday's, and go to school five days a week. That would have been all right, if I had kept it up, but I didn't for very long, I learned to read and write pretty good though. There were no Government school then that were free."

"We didn't have a name. The slaves were always known by the master's last name, and after we were freed we just took the last name of our masters and used it. After we had got our freedom papers, they had our ages and all on them, they were lost so we guess at our ages."

"Most of the slave owners were good to their slaves although some of them were brutish of course."

"In 1877 a lot of people began coming out here to Kansas, and in 1878 there were several, but in 1879 there were an awful lot of colored people immigrating. We came in 1877 to Kansas City, October 1. We landed about midnight. We came by train. Then there was nothing but little huts in the bottoms. The Santa Fe depot didn't amount to anything. The Armours' Packing house was even smaller than that. There was a swinging bridge over the river. The Kaw Valley was considered good-for-nothing, but to raise hemp. There was an awful lot of it grown there though, and there were also beavers in the Kaw River, and they used to cut down trees to build their dams. I worked several years and in 1880 I came to Franklin County."

"We raised a lot of corn, and castor beans. That was the money crop. Corn at that time wasn't hard to raise. People never plowed their corn more than three times, and they got from forty to fifty bushels per acre. There were no weeds and it was virgin soil. One year I got seventy-two bushel of corn per acre, and I just plowed it once. That may sound 'fishy' but it is true."

"There used to be a castor bean mill here, and I have seen the wagons of castor beans lined from Logan Street to First Street, waiting to unload. They had to number the wagons to avoid trouble and they made them keep their places. There also used to be a water mill here, but it burned."

"There were lots of Indians here in the Chippewas. They were harmless though. They were great to come in town, and shoot for pennies. They were good shots, and it kept you going to keep them supplied with pennies, for them to shoot with their bows and arrows, as they almost always hit them. They were always dressed in their red blankets."

"I have never used ones for work. They were used quite a bit, although I have never used them. They were considered to be good after they were broken."

"I was about twenty-two years old when I married, and I have raised six children. They live over by Appanoose. I ruined my health hauling wood. I was always a big fellow, I used to weigh over two hundred eighty-five pounds, but I worked too hard, working both summer and winter."

"My father's mother lived 'till she was around ninety or a hundred years old. She got so bent at the last she was practically bent double. She lived about two years after she was set free."

"I used to live up around Appanoose, but I came to Franklin County and I have stayed here ever since."

THE AMERICAN GUIDE
TOPEKA, KANSAS

EX SLAVE STORY
OTTAWA, KANSAS
INTERVIEWER: Leta Gray
Told by Bill Simms, ex slave, age 97 years, Ottawa, Kansas.

[TR: Information moved from bottom of last page.]

BILL SIMMS

"**M**y name is Bill Simms."

"I was born in Osceola, Missouri, March 16, 1839."

"I lived on the farm with my mother, and my master, whose name was Simms. I had an older sister, about two years older than I was. My master needed some money so he sold her, and I have never seen her since except just a time or two."

"On the plantation we raised cows, sheep, cotton, tobacco, corn, which were our principal crops. There was plenty of wild hogs, turkey, ant deer and other game. The deer used to come up and feed with the cattle in the feed yards, and we could get all the wild hogs we wanted by simply shooting them in the timber."

"A man who owned ten slaves was considered wealthy, and if he got hard up for money, he would advertise and sell some slaves, like my oldest sister was sold on the block with her children. She sold for eleven hundred dollars, a baby in her arms sold for three hundred dollars. Another sold for six hundred dollars and the other for a little less than that. My master was offered fifteen hundred dollars for me several times, but he refused to sell me, because I was considered a good husky, slave. My family is all dead, and I am the only one living.

"The slaves usually lived in a two-room house made of native lumber. The houses were all small. A four or five room house was considered a mansion. We made our own clothes, had spinning wheels and raised and combed our own cotton, clipped the wool from our sheep's backs, combed and spun it into cotton and wool clothes. We never knew what boughten clothes were. I learned to make shoes when I was just a boy and I made the shoes for the whole family. I used to chop wood and make rails and do all kinds of farm work."

"I had a good master, most of the masters were good to their slaves. When a slave got too old to work they would give him a small cabin on the plantation and have the other slaves to wait on him. They would furnish him with victuals, and clothes until he died."

"Slaves were never allowed to talk to white people other than their masters or someone their master knew, as they were afraid the white man might have the slave run away. The masters aimed to keep their slaves in ignorance and the ignorant slaves were all in favor of the Rebel army, only the more intelligent were in favor of the Union army."

"When the war started, my master sent me to work for the Confederate army. I worked most of the time for three years off and on, hauling canons, driving mules, hauling ammunition, and provisions. The Union army pressed in on us and the Rebel army moved back. I was sent home. When the Union army came close enough I ran away from home and joined the Union army. There I drove six-mule team and worked at wagon work, driving ammunition and all kinds of provisions until the war ended. Then I returned home to my old master, who had stayed there with my mother. My master owned about four hundred acres of good land, and had had ten slaves. Most of the slaves stayed at home. My master hired me to work for him. He gave my mother forty acres of land with a cabin on it and sold me a forty acres, for twenty dollars, when I could pay him. This was timbered land and had lots of good trees for lumber, especially walnut. One tree on this ground was worth one hundred dollars, if I could only get it cut and marketed, I could pay for my land. My master's wife had been dead for several years and they had no children. The nearest relative being a nephew. They wanted my master's land and was afraid he would give it all away to us slaves, so they killed him, and would have killed us if we had stayed at home. I took my mother and ran into the adjoining, Claire County. We settled there and stayed for sometime, but I wanted to see Kansas, the State I had heard so much about."

"I couldn't get nobody to go with me, so I started out afoot across the prairies for Kansas. After I got some distance from home it was all prairie. I had to walk all day long following buffalo trail. At night I would go off a little ways from the trail and lay down and sleep. In the morning I'd wake up and could see nothing but the sun and prairie. Not a house, not a tree, no living thing, not even could I hear a bird. I had little to eat, I had a little bread in my pocket. I didn't even have a pocket knife, no weapon of any kind. I was not afraid, but I wouldn't start out that way again. The only shade I could find in the daytime was the rosin weed on the prairie. I would lay down so it would throw the shade in my face and rest, then get up and go again. It was in the spring of the year in June. I came to Lawrence, Kansas, where I stayed two years working on the farm. In 1874 I went to work for a man by the month at $35 a month and I made more money than the owner did, because the grasshoppers ate up the crops. I was hired to cut up the corn for him, but the grasshoppers ate it up first. He could not pay me for sometime. Grasshoppers were so thick you couldn't step on the ground without stepping on about a dozen at each step. I got my money and came to Ottawa in December 1874, about Christmas time."

"My master's name was Simms and I was known as Simms Bill, just like horses. When I came out here I just changed my name from Simms Bill, to Bill Simms."

"Ottawa was very small at the time I came here, and there were several Indians close by that used to come to town. The Indians held their war dance on what is now the courthouse grounds. I planted the trees that are now standing on the courthouse grounds. I still planted trees until three or four years ago. There were few farms fenced and what were, were on the streams. The prairie land was all open. This is what North Ottawa was, nothing but prairie north of Logan Street, and a few houses between Logan Street and the river. Ottawa didn't have many business houses. There was also an oil mill where they bought castor beans, and made castor oil on the north side of the Marais des Cygnes River one block west of

Main Street. There was one hotel, which was called Leafton House and it stood on what is now the southwest corner of Main and Second Streets."

"I knew Peter Kaiser, when I came here, and A.P. Elder was just a boy then."

"The people lived pretty primitive. We didn't have kerosene. Our only lights were tallow candles, mostly grease lamps, they were just a pan with grease in it, and one end of the rag dragging out over the side which we would light. There were no sewers at that time."

"I had no chance to go to school when a boy, but after I came to Kansas I was too old to go to school, and I had to work, but I attended night school, and learned to read and write and figure."

"The farm land was nearly all broke up by ox teams, using about six oxen on a plow. In Missouri we lived near the Santa Fe trail, and the settlers traveling on the trail used oxen, and some of them used cows. The cows seem to stand the road better than the oxen and also gave some milk. The travelers usually aimed to reach the prairie States in the spring, so they could have grass for their oxen and horses during the summer."

"I have lived here ever since I came here. I was married when I was about thirty years old. I married a slave girl from Georgia. Back in Missouri, if a slave wanted to marry a woman on another plantation he had to ask the master, and if both masters agreed they were married. The man stayed at his owners, and the wife at her owners. He could go to see her on Saturday night and Sunday. Sometimes only every two weeks. If a man was a big strong man, neighboring plantation owners would ask him to come over and see his gals, hoping that he might want to marry one of them, but if a Negro was a small man he was not cared for as a husband, as they valued their slaves as only for what they could do, just like they would horses. When they were married and if they had children they belonged to the man who owned the woman. Osceola is where the saying originated, 'I'm from Missouri, show me.' After the war the smart guys came through and talked the people into voting bonds, but there was no railroad built and most counties paid their bonds, but the county in which Osceola stands refused to pay for their bonds because there was no railroad built, and they told the collectors to 'show me the railroad and we will pay,' and that is where 'show me' originated."

"My wife died when we had three children. She had had to work hard all her life and she said she didn't want her children to have to work as hard as she had, and I promised her on her death bed, that I would educate our girls. So I worked and sent the girls to school. My two girls both graduated from Ottawa university, the oldest one being the first colored girl to ever graduate from that school. After graduation she went to teach school in Oklahoma, but only got twenty-five dollars a month, and I had to work and send her money to pay her expenses. The younger girl also graduated and went to teach school, but she did not teach school long, until she married a well-to-do farmer in Oklahoma. The older girl got her wages raised until she got one hundred and twenty-five dollars per month. I have worked at farm work and tree husbandry all my life. My oldest daughter bought me my first suit of clothes I ever had."

"I have been living alone about twenty-five years. I don't know hew old I was, but my oldest daughter had written my mother before she died, and got our family record, which my mother kept in her old Bible. Each year she writes me and tells me on my birthday how old I am."

THE AMERICAN GUIDE
TOPEKA, KANSAS

EX SLAVE STORY
HUTCHINSON, KANSAS
INTERVIEWER: E. Jean Foote

BELLE WILLIAMS

Belle Williams was born in slavery about the year 1850 or 1851. Her mother's name was Elizabeth Hulsie, being the slave of Sid Hulsie, her last name being the name of her master. The Hulsie plantation was located in Carroll County, Arkansas. Belle Williams, better known as "Auntie Belle" is most interesting. She lives in her own little home in the one hundred block on Harvey Street, Hutchinson, Kansas. She is too old and crippled to do hard work, so spends most of her time smoking her pipe and rocking in her old armchair on the little porch of her home. She is jolly, and most interesting.

"Yes, I was a slave," she said. "I was born a slave on a plantation in Carroll County, Arkansas and lived there 'till after the war. Law sakes, honey, I can see them 'Feds' yet, just as plain as if it was yesterday. We had a long lane—you know what a lane is—well, here they come! I run for mah mammy, and I'll never forget how she grabbed me and let out a yell, "It's them Feds, them blue coats.""

"You see my massa was a good massa. He didn't

believe in whipping niggers and he didn't believe in selling niggers, and so my mammy and me, we didn't want to leave our mistress and massa. We called them 'Mother Hulsie' and 'Massa Sid.' One officer told my mammy that she could take along with her, anything out of the cabin that she wanted. Mammy looked around and said, "I don't want to take nothin' but my chillun," so we all told Mother Hulsie 'goodbye,' and when my mammy told her goodbye, why Mother Hulsie cried and cried, and said, 'I just can't let you go, Elizabeth, but go on peacefully, and maybe some day you can come back and see me.'"

As the story came word after word, big tears dropped on the thin black hands, and she reached for her tobacco can and pipe. The can was missing, so I offered to get it for her, for I was anxious for one peep into "Auntie's" little house, but I couldn't find the can, so after moans and sighs, she got to her feet and found her favorite Granger Twist. After settling; again in her chair, and when her pipe was at its best, "Auntie" continued, "Oh, honey, it was awful! You see I never been nowhere and I was scairt so I hung onto my mammy. The soldiers took us to camp that night, and after staying there several days, we went on to Springfield, Missouri, and it was right at fifty-two years ago that I came here. I was married to Fuller, my first husband and had seven chilluns. He helped me raise them that lived and, after he died, I married Williams and had two chilluns, but he didn't help me raise my chilluns. Why, honey, I raised my chilluns and my chilluns' chilluns, and even one great-grandchild now. Why, I always been a slave. I worked for all the early white families in this here town that needed help."

I asked "Auntie" if she were ever sold on the block, and she answered, "Law sakes, honey, I must tell you. No, I never was sold, but nuthin' but the Dear Blessed Lawd saved me. You see Massa Sid had gone away for a few days, and his boys was takin' care of things, when some nigger traders came and wanted to buy some niggers, and they picked on my grandmammy and me. How old was I? Well, I reckon I was about fourteen. You see, honey, I never could read or write, but I can count, and I can remember—Lawdy! how I can remember. Well, there I was on the block, just scairt and shivering—I was just cold all over—and them there nigger traders was jest a talkin', when down that long lane came Massa Sid, and I'm tellin' you, it was the Dear Lawd that sent him. He was a ridin' on his hoss, and he stopped right in front of me, standing there on the block. He looked at his boys, then he turned to them nigger traders and yelled out, "What you all doin' here?" The boys told him there was just so many niggers on the place, and they wanted some money and when the nigger traders come along they thought they would sell a few niggers. Honey, I'm tellin' you, Massa Sid turned to them nigger traders and said, "you nigger traders get out of here. These are my niggers and I don't sell niggers. I can feed them all, I don't want any help." He grabbed me right off of the block and put me on the hoss in front of him and set me down in front of my cabin. Sceered, oh Lawdy I was sceered! No, suh, Massa Sid never sold no niggers."

"I must tell you about what happened one night while we were all there in the camp. One of the massa's boys that loved my uncle, came crawling on all fours, just like a pig, into camp. He passed the pickets, and when he found my uncle he laid there on the ground in my uncle's arms and cried like a baby. My uncle was old but he cried too and after a while he told the boy that he must go back—he was 'fraid that the pickets would see him and he would be shot, so he went with him, crawling on all fours just like a pig, till he got him past the pickets, and our young master never saw my uncle any more. Oh, honey, them was heart-breakin' times. The first night we was in camp, my mammy got to thinking about Mother Hulsie and how she was left all alone with all the work, and not a soul to help her. The blue coats had gone through the house and upset everything, so in the morning she asked the captain if she could ask just one thing of him, and that was that she and my uncle go back to Mother Hulsie just for the day, and help put everything away and do the washing. The captain said they could go, but they must be back by five o'clock, and not one nigger child could go along, so they went back for the day and mammy did all the washing, every rag that she could find, and my uncle chopped and stacked outside the house, all the wood that he could chop that day, and then they came back to camp. My mammy said she'd never forget Mother Hulsie wringing her hands and crying, 'Oh Lawd, what will I do?' as they went down the land."

www.ingramcontent.com/pod-product-compliance
Lightning Source LLC
Chambersburg PA
CBHW071449040426
42445CB00012BA/1501